5 KEYS TO JOB PROMOTION

(Through The Eyes Of David And Goliath)

BY

Chayla Cooper

Table of Contents

Summary: If you want to have an unfair advantage when you go for your next job promotion, then keep reading.

Christians often separate work and faith into secular and spiritual spheres, what if there was a way to bring them together to manifest growth in your career?

In 5 Keys to Job Promotion (Through The Eyes of David and Goliath) you'll discover:

- This sure fire way to converge your experience into what your future boss is looking for
- The correct way to boost your confidence
- The exact steps to manifest your victory
- How to increase your networking capabilities
- How to BECOME before you increase your INCOME

The Bible is often referenced as standing for "Basic Instructions Before Leaving Earth". It is through this book I discovered and utilized these same key principles to gain 6 promotions in 10 years while working for the government. I know firsthand how to compete and succeed in the job market and will show you how to succeed even if you don't consider yourself religious.

Ordering Information:
Quantity sales. Special discounts are available on quantity purchases by corporations, associations, and others. For details, contact publisher at the email/website above.

CHAPTER 1
INTRODUCTION

As a Christian business coach, I am asked a lot of questions about what I actually do. I go into depth about the services I provide, teaching time management skills, improving business relationships, and reviewing and improving websites, for example, with a biblical underline in my processes. After I get a few strange looks, I then go into what being a Christian business coach is not; I do not sing hymns at every meeting, I don't pray and wish for a solution to my client's problems, and I don't shout "Amen" after every sentence. I have simply realized that many issues that plague businesses can be solved through reading the Bible combined with new-age techniques.

Once we move past the introductions, I always ask my clients this one question, what is your spiritual health like? Generally, people reply with, "Do you mean how often I go to church?" This is not what I'm asking. I'm asking for my client to check their connectivity to God from the start of our interaction because without Him, my work would be in vain.

Spiritual health is very important to the success of any business and is often overlooked when printing business cards, preparing a business plan, and answering client phone calls. So what is spiritual health? Spiritual health is our connection to the belief in a greater force (God) that provides a higher purpose. Our connectivity to God not only balances us but transcends and empowers us.

Believing we can do all things through Christ emboldens our beliefs that nothing is too hard for us to overcome. Though it is easy to get wrapped up in the day to day actions, we as believers know that we can push through anything and that God has seen this very moment where we stand and has already brought us the victory. This may sound cliche, but I know the effects of this firsthand from my career where I have climbed the corporate ladder, worked for non-profits and even started my own businesses. Sometimes, I was so stressed, I had migraines so severe that I could not see out of my left eye, would sit in my office with the lights off to work, and even the strongest prescription would not work. It wasn't until one Sunday at church, I just let go of trying to control everything and put it all in God's hands. I figured He made everything and knew all situations, so there was no need for me to stress anymore at work. No, this didn't lead to an "F-it" attitude towards my work, it was more of an "if I claim that God is the master of the universe and Christ has all powers in His hands, then I'll place my faith in Him and do my best…He'll handle the rest" attitude. And boy did that turn things around.

Growing in my spiritual health, I began to look on the inside of myself and evaluate my actions and responses to those around me. Before, I would indulge in the office gossip with coworkers, but I found myself walking away from conversations and even pausing throughout my day to pray for others. Before, I would freely express to my manager that the new policy and procedure we had to follow was crap and didn't suit the direction I was taking my unit, but after my revelation, I took a second to breathe and remember what Jesus said to the Pharisees, "Render unto Caesar, that which is Caesar's" (Matthew 22:20-22). It's not that I was taking things lying down; I just began to choose my battles and realize that certain conversations and actions were futile to my growth.

One of the most amazing effects of my new enlightenment was that I became more empathetic to those around me. It has always amazed me that we as Christ followers, can be some of the most hurtful, judgmental, and non-compassionate people in our world. My tenure as a supervisor in a welfare office helped me to not only empathize with my clients but show a greater sense of compassion towards my employees as well. In Mark 2:17, Jesus stated, "It is not the healthy who need a doctor, but the sick. I have not come to call the righteous, but the sinners." From this scripture, I looked deeper into my employees' lives and understood why we were having so many issues in production, tardiness, timeliness, and morale…they were all fighting individual battles that no one could see. When my superior only wanted disciplinary action to be taken, I took the liberty to sit my employees down one by one and addressed issues I was concerned with. Instead of immediately chastising them, I asked questions like, "How have you been?" "How's your son's college search going?" "You looked tired, is there something going on at home as to why you're not resting properly?"

Asking these compassionate questions opened up doors I never imagined. I not only took the time to listen to each problem, but I found out that one employee was tired because she just lost her home and was transitioning the children into their new environment. Another mother was coming in late due to working two jobs trying to put her child through college and hadn't adjusted to her schedule yet. While some people would take these as excuses, I found that as a supervisor, it was my duty to not only keep my customers happy but meet my employees where they were in life and ensure they could perform at the best of their ability.

Life will hit you with unexpected challenges and it will seem as if all you can do is go through the motions and pray for strength. I knew God was taking each employee through their own battle, so I made it a point to work with them to not only do the job but also to be a counselor if they needed it. From enacting a buddy system, adjusting work schedules, and showing them how to work smarter and not harder; morale boosted and I believe I had the best employees in the office...my monthly statistics also proved it *insert cocky smile here*. This could all be attributed to the hard work that my great employees and I put in, but I strongly believe that when you let go and let God work and relinquish control over every moment in your profession, He will open up your eyes and allow you to see things clearer than you ever had before. No longer from the eyes of an employee or a manager, but that of a compassionate human being who can steward over the duties that God has placed in our hands.

So why am I telling you all of this and why am I even writing this book? To help you understand one thing; your spiritual health is the key to processing your obstacles with wisdom and not out of emotions. Whether you're an entrepreneur, manager, employee, or freelancer, life will become stressful and it is no secret that people will upset you and let you down. But just like the examples I discussed, I could have easily gone the route of emotion and decided to pencil-whip my employees out the door for being late, not being focused, and poor performances. Instead, I took my emotions out of the equation and decided there had to be a logical reason behind every situation I encountered. If I had not sat my employees down one by one and discovered what was going on with their personal lives, I would have started a chain reaction that would have affected both them and I. These individuals could have been fired, suffered financially, stressed on what to do next, lose their health insurance and more.

Meanwhile, I would have to deal with downward office morale, picking up the slack until hiring someone else, a slump in timeliness, interviewing prospects, waiting months to properly train a new employee, and an increase in paperwork, time, and headaches. I'm not arguing these actions aren't necessary to take at times, sometimes you have bad apples in the bunch that need that brown box vacation, but most of the time, there is a reason behind the actions individuals take. Stepping back, removing your emotions from the situation, and seeking guidance can truly open your eyes to the situation in a new light.

One of my favorite stories in the Bible is where the Pharisees bring a woman caught in the act of adultery to Jesus and proclaim that the law of Moses states she is to be stoned to death. Fueled with emotions…and rocks, they awaited Jesus' answer on how they should handle her particular situation. Not acting quickly, the scripture says, "They were trying to trap him into saying something they could use against him, but Jesus stooped down and wrote in the dust with his finger. They kept demanding an answer, so he stood up again and said, "All right, but let the one who has never sinned throw the first stone!" (John 8:6-7) Jesus took his time to not speak out of retort but out of wisdom. The premise of thinking before you speak is loudly exemplified here and can be applied in various situations. It is not wise to rush to judgement, conclusion, or statement, but rather it is noble to pause and reflect prior to taking action. I believe that in this example, Jesus was "downloading" the sins of each man from Heaven. Directly conversing with God and writing each of their names in the dust, each one a sinner in their own right. In the conclusion of the story, the woman was released and no harm came to her as each found fault within themselves. Jesus' act of wisdom raised the condemning veil from their eyes through self reflection. You too have this gift to act in wisdom and not emotion. So, let's hone your skill together.

I hope you enjoy this book and are excited to utilize the lessons I'll teach in practicality. I wrote this book to help individuals reach the next level in their career. Whether you're looking for a promotion, career change, new to a job market, or an entrepreneur, you can take these five keys and apply them to the elevation of your career and change your life starting today. With this book, you can increase your emotional endurance, spiritual stamina, and utilize action steps to move forward in your journey. So, get your pen and paper out and get ready to take notes. God is about to move in your life. I look forward to hearing your feedback and hope you enjoy these tips.

CHAPTER 2
HAVE FAITH

So how did we get here? And how in the world will an old biblical story help me get a job promotion? I'm glad you asked.

So one day, I was driving to work, and I realized that I was stuck in a routine. Get up, sit through 30 minutes of traffic, hate my job, drive back home in traffic, and sit in my apartment numb and exhausted…just to get up and do it all again the next day. And when I say I hated my job, I HATED my job.

One Sunday afternoon, I flippantly posted on Facebook how I was dreading the start of the new week and one comment took me aback. An old college friend wrote under my post, "your situation won't change until you do. God won't bless you with more unless he knows you are appreciative and can handle what you have now."

After reading her comment, I won't lie, I mocked her. "Yea, yea, yea, I know." I continued to go about my day and bask in all of the comments in agreement with me. But you know God has a funny way of pulling on your mind and heart. I kept feeling this urge to open my Bible throughout the day. Finally, before bed, I gave in and picked up my Bible and pulled one of those movie scene moves and just turned to a random page and read. Lo and behold, the story of David and Goliath stared me right in my face.

David is one of the best characters in the Bible. An unsuspecting young man rising through the ranks to become the second king of the new nation of Israel. Channeling the glory that our God can provide, yet still human enough to share his mistakes with us. I draw so much from his testimony. But what I love about his defeating of Goliath is the fortitude he showed in the face of every obstacle placed in front of him, and how his faith and love for God brought him through. It is through David that I discovered the keys to unlocking the next level in my life.

One of the first things I picked up from this story is that you have to have faith. Once you decide to step into a new position and leave the old behind, believe that you can do what you're setting out to do. I follow a lot of entrepreneurs online and one of the first things they always say is that before you start on a new journey, write down your goals and believe

7

you can do it. No one is standing in your way but you, so you have to decide every day that you will see this through. Whether that requires you to go back to school to gain a higher degree or certificate, baptize yourself into *"Youtube University"* to learn new software, or watch webinars on how to improve your marketing skills, it all starts with your belief that you are meant for greater than what your eyes see. I'm not stating this for motivational purposes... this is the truth.

David was the youngest of his father's eight sons and was sent to the battle lines to bring rations to his brothers who were of fighting age. While in the camp, David overheard Goliath's boasting of how he would defeat the Israelites and rule over them. Often called "A man after God's own heart," David would not stand by as a foreigner disrespected his creator.

Now picture this; a teenage boy with no battle experience declares to an entire army...no, an entire nation, that he will defeat the one enemy standing between them and being conquered completely. Imagine the faith and reassurance this young man had to have to stand up to the greatest challenge he has encountered. And it's one thing for David to have faith and keep it to himself, but this story would have never been written if he didn't speak his future into existence and know without a shadow of a doubt that the Lord had his back.

In 1 Samuel 17:32, we find David speaking with Saul, the first king of Israel, "Let no one lose heart on account of this Philistine; your servant will go and fight him." The significance of this moment can go by so quickly. A child, speaking to his elder-an authority figure, is encouraging them to have peace and to stand on his word. It's as if David knew something that Saul didn't...or forgot, that the victory was already won and there wasn't anything to fear.

Driving to work, hating my job, feeling numb to my surroundings... I lost heart. I lost the passion I had when I first got the job. I lost the fire that told me I was making a difference. My vision was deterred from seeing the joy and fruitfulness of each task, and I lost the faith that God was taking me to the promised land, perpetually stuck in what felt like the wilderness.

As I continued to read, David's faith continued to be sprinkled throughout the pages. 1 Samuel 17:43-44 shows the dialogue between

Goliath and our protagonist: "He said to David, 'Am I a dog, that you come at me with sticks?' And the Philistine cursed David by his gods. 'Come here,' he said, 'and I'll give your flesh to the birds and the wild animals!' " But the mighty proclamation that David replied with is legendary. "You come against me with sword and spear and javelin, but I come against you in the name of the Lord Almighty, the God of the armies of Israel, whom you have defied. This day the Lord will deliver you into my hands, and I'll strike you down and cut off your head. This very day I will give the carcasses of the Philistine army to the birds and the wild animals, and the whole world will know that there is a God in Israel. All those gathered here will know that it is not by sword or spear that the Lord saves; for the battle is the Lord's, and he will give all of you into our hands." The epitome of faith talk.

Again, David was a child in the eyes of the land, had no formal military training, and was counted out by everyone around him, even his own family. Yet, he spoke with such reassurance, gumption, and vigor that despite everything around him telling him that he's not prepared, he's not worthy, he's not capable, and to go home, he stood firm on the truth that the battle isn't his alone to fight, but it's the Lord's. And the Lord is always victorious.

Have you forgotten the battles the Lord has brought you through? We, as the mere mortals we are, forget to have trust in the Lord that has prepared a way for us on numerous occasions. Like seriously, how many occasions can you think of where God has kept you healthy, rescued you from death, kept you safe, even come through on a test when your eyes glazed over? Too many times to count. And even if you "don't believe," how many times have you said this infamous prayer, "Lord, if you just get me out of this, I promise I'll never..."? You do this because that twinge in the back of your neck knows that you are reigned by a higher power and that calling on God will manifest your request into existence.

Faith is said to be the evidence of things hoped for and not yet seen. This simply means you must see it in your mind before you see it in your line of sight. Seek the Lord and tell Him the desires of your heart and watch Him prepare a way for you through your wilderness. Claim your victory right here, right now. Declare with your tongue the faith that you have in God, that He will continue to bless you and has great things prepared for you.

Jeremiah 29:11-13 states, "For I know the plans I have for you," declares the Lord, "plans to prosper you and not to harm you, plans to give you hope and a future. Then you will call on me and come and pray to me, and I will listen to you. You will seek me and find me when you seek me with all your heart." So just know, where you are right now, is nowhere compared to the beautiful places God will take you. So the real question now is, are you ready to go on this ride?

CHAPTER 3
YOU ARE PREPARED

Ok, so you have faith, you believe you can do it, you're pumped up and you're going to pull the trigger and apply for the job online. Your confidence is overflowing, until you reach the qualifications section of the posting and your heart sinks.

"I can't do this!"

"What is this?"

"I've never even heard of that program!"

I want you to step back from the computer, take a deep breath, and I want you to know this one thing…you are prepared. Regardless of whatever is on that posting, what your mind is telling you, maybe even through the negativity of your peers…you are prepared.

Our God has a funny way of utilizing things we say or think are insignificant and turning them into the very tools we need at the right moment.

Going back to David and Goliath, 1 Samuel 17:34-37, David shares with Saul how God has tested and prepared him for this very moment.

"Your servant has been keeping his father's sheep. When a lion or a bear came and carried off a sheep from the flock, I went after it, struck it and rescued the sheep from its mouth. When it turned on me, I seized it by its hair, struck it and killed it. Your servant has killed both the lion and the bear; this uncircumcised Philistine will be like one of them because he has defied the armies of the living God. The Lord who rescued me from the paw of the lion and the paw of the bear will rescue me from the hand of this Philistine."

Can you imagine having the courage to fight a bear with your bare hands? David cannot be any more than one hundred fifty pounds soaking wet, coming up against a 500-pound bear that could easily tear him apart, and yet, God allows him to be swift enough to strike and kill a beast that can run on average 20 miles per hour. And not just one time, he states how he's killed both beasts, the lion and the bear. Step back and picture it, the stale air of mud emanating from the ground, the hairs raised on the back of David's neck, the glare of death from the lion as blood drips from his mouth, all while David is shaking on the inside. Who lunges first? I suspect David in my mind because he knows he can't go home without a good story of why he has one less lamb in his flock. Maneuvering his feet on the wet ground to control his stance, utilizing his enemy's strength against them, knowing when and where to strike to end the fight…this wasn't just a battle for a sheep, this was training, and David had just entered God's gym whether he was ready or not.

Now as you recall, I made it very clear that I hated my job. So much so, that I even told my boss I hated my job after she called me into her office and stated that she noticed my countenance was lower than normal. I expressed that I felt that my education and talent was being wasted and I found the work she was giving me to be "busy work" that could be handed off to her secretary. Her brilliant remedy to counter my disdain was to place me as the head of the morale committee. Her logic was, if I could make my work environment happier for me, then it'll trickle down to the employees underneath me. You can imagine the thrill I had inside. But I picked up the ball and ran with it, all the while remembering, "your situation won't change unless you do."

I kept analyzing data I felt was mundane and tedious. I kept running down supervisors for reports. I kept implementing procedures to address the office's timeliness issue. All the while trying my best to keep a smile on my face and tell myself that, "this is significant." Until one day, just as with David, I was thrust into my destiny.

I was contacted by my Program Manager's assistant and asked if I would like to interview for the supervisor position I applied for months ago. The joy that shot from my face is something that I'll never forget. I accepted the invitation and went into our job portal and printed off the job posting so I could study for the interview and be prepared…so I thought.

I went home that night and read over the job description and qualifications carefully. Now I knew that I had an educational advantage over some of my peers, and as an assistant manager, I have stepped into the role as supervisor numerous times when called upon. But something in the bottom of my chest told me I was not equipped for this next step on the career ladder. I was not capable. I was not smart enough. I closed my eyes and took several deep breaths as I laid in bed with sheets of paper thrown across my comforter. As I opened my eyes, I looked to my right and saw my bible laying beside me as if God himself placed it there as a subtle reminder to lean on His word. I turned to 1 Samual and reread the story of David and Goliath and with each word, my assurance swelled larger and larger. I can do this.

I walked into the Regional office on the day of my interview feeling hopeful. Not only did I pray and prepare in the days leading up, but an assortment of familiar faces greeted me as I walked the halls to the cubicle where I would review the questions before being blasted with questions from the firing squad of Program Managers. As I jotted down bullet points to organize my thoughts on how I would answer the questions, I said one simple prayer; "Lord, if this be your will, let it be so."

I walked into the conference room with my shoulders back and head held high. After I shook the hands of my interviewers, I sat in my seat. Squirming to find just the right position that would hold me for the next twenty to thirty minutes, I settled and took a sip of water from my water bottle, let out one silent breath, and locked in…it was game time.

My immediate supervisor was in the room and stated that she would not be taking notes during my time, as to recuse herself from showing any bias within the hiring process. I nodded in affirmation and took my first question from the Regional Director. Repeatedly, I gave three to four examples to each question to demonstrate my experience and knowledge. I caught myself speaking so fast that I paused and asked if they needed me to slow down. As the Regional Director made a joke about how between the three of them, they should be able to piece together my answers, I looked over to my supervisor and noticed how she was sitting back in her chair with her arms crossed…smiling at me. A sense of reassurance rushed through me as I continued to barrel through the last few questions.

After my interview, I returned to my office to fulfill my duties as an assistant manager and cover for a supervisor that was out for the day. As I was sitting in my office catching up on emails, I got a phone call from my manager.

"What are you doing?"

"Umm, working."

"Do you have a minute?"

"Yes ma'am…"

"Are you sitting down?"

"Umm, yes ma'am."

"I would like to offer you the position of supervisor for our north office…"

I bowed my head and cried immediately.

"Chayla, are you there?"

"Oh, yes, ma'am, I'm here," I said with a cracked voice.

"Well, do you accept my offer?" she asked as she laughed.

"Yes, ma'am, I do! Thank you so much for your time today and this opportunity." I smiled and fought to say through the tears and snot running down my face.

"You were the most detailed candidate we interviewed. I never had someone provide as many examples as you did for any position. You earned this."

As we concluded our conversation, I hung up the phone, stood up to close the door to my office, turned around to face the window, fell to my knees and cried. In a low tone, I said thank you repeatedly as I lifted my hands to God in complete gratitude. My Lord took every report I pulled in disdain and turned it into my ability to analyze data. He took my daily troubleshooting of the system and turned it into my familiarity with the software. My God took the checkout process I created to ensure employees completed their cases timely and turned it into an ability to problem solve and manage others with time-sensitive information. I was being groomed in the wilderness for this one moment to shine, just as David, and just like you.

There's a saying, "you can't have a testimony without a test." God must refine you in the fire of life to get you to learn and develop the skills He needs you to have for when He's ready to take you to the next level. Everything that you have gone through was only preparation for your purpose. Take each action, each step, each email, each report, every rude customer, and before you get aggravated, compartmentalize the situation and remember that everything is significant to your journey. Flip the negativity on its head and use it for the good of the Lord.

One of my favorite scriptures is Romans 8:28, "And we know that all things work together for the good to them that love the Lord, to them who are called according to his purpose." The bible says, "all things work together," that entails the good and the bad. The fun and the hard. The confusion and the knowledge. It all comes together for your good, for your triumph, and for His glory. You already have the job promotion you crave, you just have to gather all of the pieces to present it.

Picture this, you wouldn't eat garlic by itself, would you? What about an onion? You wouldn't just bite down into an onion for a snack. And I know you wouldn't just take a glass of olive oil and sip on it as you watch television in the evening. These things separately are not appetizing, but bring them together with ground beef, crushed tomatoes, fresh parsley, oregano, and some salt and pepper and you just made a delicious spaghetti sauce. All things, the tasty and the eye-watering, come together for the good of the meal. Nothing is wasted or insignificant, and every ingredient plays a role. Think of this when you apply for your next position, everything you have gone through to this point has played a role in the great employee that you are. Your compassion when dealing with irate customers has made you great at conflict resolution. Your tenacity and speed in finishing your work ahead of schedule showcases your ability to manage your time effectively. Your collective gathering of mundane spreadsheets and explaining your conclusions to your superior has made you a great data analyst. Take your experiences and flip them on their head and see how God has prepared you for the next level.

CHAPTER 4
BELIEVE YOU HAVE THE VICTORY

So you have faith and the belief that God has prepared you for your journey. You have placed all of your hopes and dreams in His hands, expecting Him to make a way out of no way. But God requires a partnership. This is a fundamental key that God shows us from creation. When God created Adam and Eve, He said for them to "Be fruitful and multiply; fill the earth and subdue it. Rule over the fish in the sea and the birds in the sky and over every living creature that moves on the ground" (Genesis 1:28). Now God surely does not need our help to do anything, please always remember that, but it is in His loving generosity that He wishes to partner with us and make us feel part of the process. Requiring us to work for what we want and to rule over our dominion. So I have one question, are you a worker or a ruler?

I know you want the promotion, but how are you approaching it? Are you applying and looking at the interview process as just another employee trying to climb the corporate ladder? Or do you see where you want to go and this ladder is in your way, so you smash any obstacle that gets in your way as you place one foot in front of the other? Are you owning each step with precision of where you want to be?

James 2:14, 17 states, "What good is it, dear brothers and sisters, if you say you have faith but don't show it by your actions? So you see, faith by itself isn't enough. Unless it produces good deeds, it is dead and useless." God created us to not just wish, hope and cry out to Him to change our situations, but empowered us to take action and dominion over things in our control. This next step in your life isn't just your request for more pay and responsibilities; no, this is your step out of what no longer serves you. You have decided to change the view and circumstances around you for the better and now you have to claim the victory.

Remember when David asked for Saul's permission to face Goliath, he wasn't just asking to face a person, this boy was asking the king of Israel could he promote from shepherd boy to soldier. From the lowest of professions to a man of stature who potentially could marry the king's daughter if he survived. David didn't mince words either, "Let no one lose heart on account of this Philistine; your servant will go and fight him." Determination, grounded in his abilities, and confidence leaps from the page. David had never even stepped onto a battlefield before, but it didn't matter. He was assured of his abilities and it didn't matter the setting you put him in, he knew that he would come out victorious.

Back to 1 Samuel 17: 34-37; when David shared with Saul his informal training of fighting the bear and the lion, it was as if David was saying, "I've seen this before and I know how to win." What have you seen before that you know without a shadow of a doubt that no matter what this next position throws at you, you know you will knock it out with precision?

Constantly dealing with rude customers? That's years of experience in conflict resolution. Phishing through reports to discover a common thread to a problem? That's data analysis experience. Proofreading emails and other notices before they're presented to the masses? That's copywrite experience. Growing your online profile to over one thousand people in a month? That's social media marketing experience. These are just a few examples, but no matter what your background is, when it comes down to the battlefield of life, can you adapt your training to suit the enemy before you?

God has heard your cries, counted every tear, trained you in obscurity, and has delivered you from every obstacle before you. Step back, look around you and think back to where you were a few months ago…a few years ago, aren't you glad to be standing where you are today? So if you know that He is a deliverer and can pull you through anything, take up your sling and know that He will do it again and again. You have the victory, you are a conqueror, and above all else, you are a child of God. Now act like it.

CHAPTER 5
HE'LL PLACE YOU WHERE YOU NEED TO BE FOR BETTER NETWORKING

I'm sure if you're reading this, that you're old enough to know the mantra, "it's not what you know but who you know." Well, I can 100% attest to this. This is not only true from a spiritual standpoint, but in the physical realm as well.

It is my assumption that by picking up this book, you associate yourself with Christ, Christianity, and/or God and wish to transfer your faith into physical manifestation. To even connect with my original point of having faith, you must believe in at least one out of the three. When you pray and ask for things, you're not just stating them out for "whomever" to complete, you're banking on having a relationship with God, and in that relationship you have reassurance that whatever you ask shall come to pass. It's in this relationship that you hold onto the notion that you are one of God's children, manifested in His image, that you can come to Him in humility and boldness and whatever you ask for will be given unto you. Without this connection, there wouldn't be faith, religion, or a relationship with the heavens. So if you know that your connection with God is your foundation to manifestation, what makes you think that your earthly connections aren't as important?

From the very beginning with the creation of Adam, God said that it was not good for him to be alone. Creating Eve formed a connection between the two that would carry them through the wilderness they set upon themselves. It was the familial and blood connection between Moses, the Hebrews, and his adoption into the palace that made him the perfect intercessor to free the Israelites from pharaoh's grasp. And following his father's orders placed David into the right room, at the right time, with the right people to thrust him into his destiny.

1 Samuel 17:17-19 tells us that Jesse, David's father, simply wanted him to take supplies to his brothers and to send back news of their wellbeing. "Now Jesse said to his son David, "Take this ephah of roasted grain and these ten loaves of bread for your brothers and hurry to their camp. Take along these ten cheeses to the commander of their unit. See how your brothers are and bring back some assurance from them. They

are with Saul and all the men of Israel in the Valley of Elah, fighting against the Philistines."

I always laugh at the thought of an obedient teenager doing as their father pleases without griping and complaining…this was truly a different time. But digging into the scripture, David, the mere shepherd boy, was told by his father to not only go see his brothers but also to take cheese to the commander of their unit. A simple gift, I imagine, for keeping his older sons safe, or was it a set up by God to establish a deeper connection? We know that David will one day become king, an excellent soldier, and whose name will echo throughout the ages, but David, through following a father's simple instruction, is placed in uncharted territory among the men he will soon lead. He doesn't know this, but the God that has weaved time itself knew what was needed to get him to where he needed to be. God will do this for you as well. That sudden urge to buy donuts for the office, accepting lunch with a fellow coworker, filling in for a sick coworker, it is in the everyday mundane actions that God builds connections for you with the right people. And it is in His timing that these relationships flourish, and you will one day understand the purpose of each step you took to get to where you always wanted to go.

David did as instructed by his earthly father and delivered the provisions to his brothers and their commander. In doing so, he admonished the foul narrative of Goliath in front of the entire camp, catching the ears of soldiers, commanders, messengers, and even the king of Israel himself, Saul. 1 Samuel 17:31-32 shares, "What David said was overheard and reported to Saul, and Saul sent for him. David said to Saul, "Let no one lose heart on account of this Philistine; your servant will go and fight him."

Three things we can learn from these verses; one, you never know who overhears what you're saying and how it can thrust you into your destiny, second, your name is being spoken in rooms you haven't even stepped into yet, and third, when God is ready to promote you to the next level, you'll be sent for. Keeping these key points in mind will not only change the way you see a job promotion, as something you should chase after, but through your everyday actions, words, and connections with people, realize that you are planting the seeds for your future.

Remember, David is just a shepherd boy who is now rubbing shoulders with the king and had no idea what that this day would bring such a shift in his life. One minute he's in the field tending to his sheep, the next, a crowded campsite with battle lines drawn and his destiny staring him in the face. I have experienced this phenomenon in my life on numerous occasions, and what I have learned is to trust God when you get a chance to be in "the" room. Your work ethic, reputation, and faith have already preceded you before you stepped into the room. You have already claimed the victory in speaking promotion into your life and working as diligently as if for the Lord (Colossians 3:23), now is the time to step into your destiny with your head held high and the confidence in which we are entitled. Remember, you are the child of a king, the king of kings! And according to His riches and glory, He will give you exceedingly abundantly above all that you ask for (Ephesians 3:20-21). So when the call comes, and trust me, it will, think to yourself, "I've prayed for this, so I'm made for this." Now go charge that battlefield and take what's yours.

CHAPTER 6
BE YOURSELF

Before you dismiss the cliche of the title of this chapter, I want you to know one thing; there is only one you and that is your advantage in gaining a promotion. Only you have had the experiences that have given you the knowledge you possess, only you have found particular creative ways to solve problems, only you are on the path that God has for you!

God shows us this notion when Saul tries to force his style of battle preparation onto David. 1 Samuel 17:38-40 shares with us, "Then Saul dressed David in his own tunic. He put a coat of armor on him and a bronze helmet on his head. David fastened on his sword over the tunic and tried walking around, because he was not used to them. 'I cannot go in these,' he said to Saul, 'because I am not used to them.' So he took them off. Then he took his staff in his hand, chose five smooth stones from the stream, put them in the pouch of his shepherd's bag and, with his sling in his hand, approached the Philistine."

Saul tried to force what he knew about winning battles onto David: his tunic, sword, and armor. This is how Saul was trained to fight his battles. When David attempted to put on Saul's armor, trying to be someone he was not, his breath was stifled by the helmet, he was weighed down from the armor, and constricted in movement from the sword around his waist...unable to provide his best as he was confined by his environment. It was only when he remembered that he got into the audience of the king by being himself and returning to what he was used to, did David champion in battle. By the time David learned how to operate outside of his norm, the battle would have been lost and over. He knew that to claim the victory, he would have to rely on what instinctively came natural to him.

How often have you been at work and wondered why things weren't running as smoothly as they could? And when you suggested to management or a tenured employee a new outlook on how to deliver a process, they give you this same old line, "that's just how it's always been done." Or this other nugget, "if it ain't broke, don't fix it." This has always puzzled me because is it not the job of a company to change with the times and to stay relevant? I've experienced this often in my career and still shined through my unique talents.

I hold a bachelor of arts in Film and Digital media from Baylor University, I have written and published music for years, I have children's books available for purchase, and I'm what some consider a millennial. My strength is that I am vulnerable when I tell a story. In a culture that says to worry about themselves, I share music about falling in love, heartbreak, and self empowerment. My children books are a cross between Christian guidance and societal change. My purpose in this book series is to express how my intersection of Christian values and business acumen has led me to success for over a decade. I am a complex mixture of this world and the next and it is in my freedom of transference that I provide my best to the world. I am the same person you'll meet in person, in my music, and in my books. I draw on this in confidence that God only made one of me and when I step into a room, no one has the experiences and talents I possess…I already have the victory.

In a previous position of mine, it was my duty to train supervisors on how to properly transfer employees to new offices and to terminate their permissions within our online system. At first, I went along with the methodology and observed my mentor in a few sessions to see how the information was to be taught. But it always puzzled me why we constantly would receive emails, calls, and help desk tickets from these same individuals who recently took the class, citing that they could not follow the processes we spent nearly two hours explaining. I looked at the training materials we gave attendees at the end of the class for reference and realized that I wouldn't want to read over the information either! It was only a few word documents filled with paragraphs and bullet points. My eyes glazed over in boredom by just looking at it myself. So, I took the initiative and asked my supervisor if it was ok if I revamped the training materials by providing screenshots and other visual effects that drew the eye to pertinent information. At first, there was a slight tug of war with some on my team because of that adage, "if it ain't broke, don't fix it," but in the end, we dug into the trenches together and created a work we were all proud of. Don't be afraid to utilize your strengths to shine through and shake up the status quo, you don't know who is depending on you to bring about the change only your mind can provide.

22

Hebrews 12:1-2 tells us that God has marked out a particular path for each of us and it is ours to run alone. "Therefore, since we are surrounded by such a great cloud of witnesses, let us throw off everything that hinders and the sin that so easily entangles. And let us run with perseverance the race marked out for us, fixing our eyes on Jesus, the pioneer and perfecter of faith." You cannot be anyone else but yourself in the kingdom of God. When God knitted you together in your mother's womb, He only made one of you. Merging together your exact strengths and weaknesses, He knew where you would fall short, Jesus, Himself, and the holy spirit will pick up the slack. I say this because if you're not careful to rejoice in all that you are, you will let the cloak of envy hide you from your blessing.

"When the men were returning home after David had killed the Philistine, the women came out from all the towns of Israel to meet King Saul with singing and dancing, with joyful songs and with timbrels and lyres. As they danced, they sang: "Saul has slain his thousands, and David his tens of thousands." Saul was very angry; this refrain displeased him greatly. "They have credited David with tens of thousands," he thought, "but me with only thousands. What more can he get but the kingdom?" And from that time on Saul kept a close eye on David…Saul was afraid of feared David, because the Lord was with David but had departed from Saul." Expressed through 1 Samuel 18:6-9, 12.

Many scholars like to stop the story of David and Goliath at the fall of the giant and the victory of the unsuspecting shepherd boy, but on the other side of victory is always adversity. When you gain a promotion, you have more responsibilities. You have a child, you must raise them for eighteen years. You get a house, and you have to come out of pocket for upkeep and other expenses. David slew the Philistine, but unexpectedly gained an enemy in his King. Instead of rejoicing in his loyal servant defeating the problem that plagued his nation, Saul shifted his eyes in jealousy and raged because he wasn't as celebrated as David. Not focusing on himself led to his imminent downfall.

Now Saul knew well this was David's first time on the battlefield and that Goliath was his first kill but hearing the false report of those around him made his countenance shift from celebration to contemplation. When seeking a new position, there will be competition and speculations swirling around those participating. This person may have more degrees than you, this person may have more years at the company than you, this one may have built a stronger connection with the managers, but it all does not matter. Your focus is to be true to yourself and to run the race that God has set before you. What God has for you, no one can take away, keep from you, or deter you from it. The negative and distracting words from those around you are only steppingstones for you to build your trust in the Father.

And what if you don't get this particular promotion you are striving for? Can you trust in God and know that what He has for you is better than what you can physically see? Saul blocked not only his blessings but the very communication he had with God because of his own jealousy and shortsightedness. Verse twelve stated, "Saul was afraid of David, because the Lord was with David but had departed from Saul." In the same day, within the span of what I can only imagine is between eight to twelve hours, the king on the throne went from encouraging his servant to tackle his enemy to fearing him and then dug himself deeper into a hole and stated that the creator of the heavens and earth has left him. Instead of appreciating the gift of a strong soldier that David was to become, Saul tormented and persecuted the person who was there to punish all that tormented him. If you are met with disappointment, will you trust the path that the Father has for you and continue to strive forward with your head held high? Or will you become disheartened and lash out in fear that God has left you?

Stay true to yourself and all that God has for you. In this day and age of social media, it's easy to see what others may be accomplishing, and you may think that you're not progressing as fast as those you know. One key fact to remember, everyone online is showing you their highlight reel and not their entire movie. You may see your high school sweetheart with a husband and new baby, but you don't know how many nights they cried when they discovered they could not conceive. Your best friend may have received a new home, but you don't know how many banks denied him before he got serious about fixing his credit. Your coworker may post herself running a marathon, but you don't know that she's doing so in remembrance of a loved one that passed away, and every day she battles with grief. Your race is your own, and as long as you continue to be yourself and cherish your own talents, God will continue to shine His light on your hopes, dreams and ambitions.

CHAPTER 7
ACTION ITEMS

There you have it, the five keys you must possess to get a job promotion as illustrated through the old testament story of David and Goliath. To recap, you must have faith, know that you are prepared, believe you have the victory, know that God will increase your network, and be yourself. Once you have these points buried in your mind and heart, your spiritual stamina will sustain you as you go through the process of applying for higher positions.

James 2:17 shares with us that "...faith by itself, if it is not accompanied by action, is dead." As much as I appreciate you taking the time to read my words, you didn't pick up this book to simply get a rush of motivation, only to go back to feeling and doing the same thing. So here are action items that you can take with you to help you build your confidence, trust in God, and strive for your best self:

- Pray
- Write down your intentions
- Speak your faith into existence
- Pay attention to your surroundings
- Work on self-improving

Prayer is the prime source of communication between our earthly dwelling and the unseen heavens. It is our acknowledgment of God that we know He is there and in control, and in this truth, we worry less. Philippians 4:6-7 shares the rewards of relinquishing our strife to the Lord, "Do not be anxious about anything, but in every situation, by prayer and petition, with thanksgiving, present your requests to God. And the peace of God, which transcends all understanding, will guard your hearts and your minds in Christ Jesus." I don't know about you, but I love to delegate hard task to others. Who better to give my burdens to than the one person we have ever labeled "The Prince of Peace."

Writing down your aspirations is not only the fastest way to guarantee their arrival, but to also mark the time and date that God shows up in His unexpected way. "Write the vision down and make it plain, so that one may read it in a hurry. This vision is for a future time. It describes the end, and it will be fulfilled. If it seems slow in coming, wait patiently, for it will surely take place. It will not be delayed." Reads Habakkuk 2:2-3. Our God stands on His word, for it is His word that keeps the stars in the sky, the earth on its axis, and the breath inside our lungs. Knowing this within our hearts, once we write down our dreams, God will literally move heaven and earth to fulfill your desires according to His riches and glory...and last time I checked, there was no shortage of wealth in Heaven. So from His coffers, your cup shall overflow with goodness and abundance.

I've already shared how David spoke in faith on that fateful day to call down the strength of God over the enemy of the chosen people of Israel. Now, it is your turn to witness to yourself and speak to what you wish to appear before your very eyes. Declare out loud that you have the promotion, you have financial peace of mind, that you have the victory over uncertainty. You are a victor, not a victim. Approach each step of your journey with this mindset and remember that even when the battle may seem to be lost, your God has never lost a war.

Now God will place you around the right people at the right time to expand your network, as I have demonstrated...but are you paying attention? Are your eyes open to the influence that surrounds you? Do not read this and think to only look at those around you as mere steppingstones to reach a higher level, but build an actual friendship with others because you don't know who God will use to not only bless you, but your bloodline as well. Hebrews 13:2 states, "Don't forget to show hospitality to strangers, for some who have done this have entertained angels without realizing it!" Favor and karma may not be sisters, but I'm sure their cousins. We are all strings in this tapestry we call life, building strong relationships not only will help widen your network, but makes us stronger in the body of Christ. Nobody can go at it alone, and remember, you don't have to.

Not only has God showed me this key through reading His word, He laid it ever so nicely in my lap one day when I went on a job interview. I remember being walked into a conference room where I was given a few minutes to myself before the manager would be available to see me. I said my usual prayer, "Lord, if this is for me, let it be according to your will.

If it is not, let me gain knowledge from it," when suddenly, the supervisor came through the door like a whirlwind, expressing her apologies for being late. After a brief shaking of hands and exchange of pleasantries, I prepared to accept my first question, when she threw me for a curveball and asked if I was from Houston, Texas. Taken aback, I said "Yes, though I had not lived there in ten years." She asked if I knew a woman named Cynthia Cooper and if she worked in the medical field. I again stated yes, but now I sat confused as to how she would know all of this. It turns out, she and my mother used to be coworkers and she had nothing but admirable things to say about the time she spent with her. Whatever nerves I had going into the interview were now gone and I was basking in the peace that this connection my mother built unknowingly, was showing up through God's hand in another season.

Your last action item is to always work on improving your skills. The world is changing and with the availability of the internet, it is easier than ever to access free information to keep your skills up to date in a competitive market. God wants us to mold the gifts He has given us, to use them for His glory, and to serve those around us.

David spent hours in the field playing his lyre among the sheep. It was due to those hours of solitude and practice he gained the reputation of being the best player in the land. 1 Samuel 16: 14-23 shares with us a time before Goliath came to torment Israel. Instead we find Saul tormented by what he calls and evil spirit. The servants ask the king in verse 16, "Your Majesty, why don't you command us to look for a man who can play the lyre well?" Wishing to find any semblance of relief, Saul agrees, "Please find me a man who can play well and bring him to me." One of the officials said, "I know one of Jesse's sons from Bethlehem who can play well. He's a courageous man and a warrior. He has a way with words, he is handsome, and the Lord is with him." And yet again, David is sent for, leading back to the points from chapter five; your name is spoken in rooms you haven't stepped in, God will place you with people that may benefit your future, and you never know who is listening to you.

I wish you many blessings on your quest for a brighter future. As I release this, I pray that each and every one of you that picks this manuscript up will gain the insight and guidance that God has for you. Matthew 7:7-8 states, "Ask and it will be given to you; seek and you will find; knock and the door will be opened to you. For everyone who asks receives; the one who seeks finds; and to the one who knocks, the door will be opened." The Lord who commands the winds and the waves has heard your earnest prayers and sees your quest to seek better for yourself. Have faith and don't lose heart; your victory is coming in Jesus' name. I speak this in agreeance with you and wish you a blessed and fruitful life.

FREE GIFT

There you have it! Five keys to your next job promotion and five action items you can implement today.

As I initially stated, I'm a Christian Business Coach, and I would be remiss to not give you keen knowledge on your quest for a new promotion. So as a thank you for your time in reading my work, I would like to offer you a free resume review to start you on your journey to a brighter future.

Resumakeover specializes in rejuvenating resumes, cover letters, and LinkedIn profiles. Their professionalism is unmatched and their services are fast and affordable.

To claim your gift, go to www.chaylacooper.com/freeoffer. Input your name and email address and you're on your way!